DRAW 3-D

A step-by-step guide to perspective drawing

D0730989

by

Doug DuBosque

WITHDRAWN

ꜰꝋPEEL
Growing books for growing people!

Introduction

3-D means "three dimensional."

It's easy to draw from side to side on your paper, using its **width.** It's easy to draw from top to bottom on your paper, using its **height.** But how do you draw something going away from you, into the distance? How do you create **depth** (the third dimension) in your drawing?

The answer you'll find here is *linear perspective,* a technique of drawing first developed almost 500 years ago, during the Renaissance.

As you flip through the pages of this book, it may all look sort of complicated and technical. And it is...sort of. Those clever artists who figured this all out weren't trying to make it simple. They were trying to make their pictures look real.

Fortunately, the basics are pretty simple. And you don't need much beyond the basics to make some pretty cool drawings. Best of all, perspective can make your drawings look real in a way you can't achieve without it.

You'll need a few supplies, some patience and a positive attitude. If I mess up perspective drawings after years of experience (and I do), you can probably expect a few disasters as you learn...just smile and go with the flow: after all, with each mistake you learn another way *not* to do it!

The best way to learn is to do, so grab a pencil and get started!

What you need...

Find a comfortable place to draw – with decent light, so you can see what you're doing.

1. A mechanical pencil works best for this type of drawing.
2. Have a ruler or straightedge handy. It's very difficult to draw in perspective without one.
3. If you have one, use a T-square and triangle.
4. You'll probably want a separate eraser (the eraser on your pencil will disappear quickly). My favorite type is a kneaded type, available in art supply and craft stores.
5. Patience: pay attention to the concepts. Do plenty of practice drawings!

Copyright ©1999 Douglas C. DuBosque.

All rights reserved, including the right of reproduction in whole or in part, in any form.

Published by Peel Productions, Inc.

Manufactured in the United States of America

Library of Congress Cataloging-in-Publication Data

DuBosque, D. C.
    Draw 3-D : step by step perspective drawing / by Doug DuBosque
        p. cm.
    Summary: Provides instructions for making perspective drawings.
    ISBN 0-939217-14-7
    1. Perspective--juvenile literature. 2. Drawing--Technique--juvenile literature.
    [1. Perspective. 2. Drawing--Technique.] I. Title. II. Title: Draw 3D.
NC750.D87   1998
742--dc21   98-42174

Distributed to the trade and art markets in North America by

NORTH LIGHT BOOKS,
an imprint of F&W Publications, Inc.
4700 East Galbraith Road
Cincinnati, OH 45236

(800) 289-0963

Contents

The starting point 4

Your name in 3-D 8

Draw a box in 3-D 10

Two boxes, one vanishing point 11

Four boxes, one vanishing point 13

More depth with a vanishing point 14

The horizon (eye level) 15

Perspective in action: a road 16

Perspective in action: an interior 26

Dividing spaces evenly 32

A bridge 34

Two-point perspective 36

A ramp 38

Vanishing points and camera lenses 42

More about the horizon and eye level 44

Curved objects in 3-D 46

A 3-D checkerboard 48

Perspective in action: a house 50

Adding shadows in 3-D 55

More shadows in 3-D 58

3-point perspective 60

Another way to divide space 61

4-point perspective? .62

Multiple Vanishing points 63

The starting point

1. Draw six circles.

2. Make a dot somewhere in the middle of the circles.

   In 3-D drawing, this is called the <u>vanishing point</u>.

Vanishing point: where lines going away from you in the drawing come together, or converge.

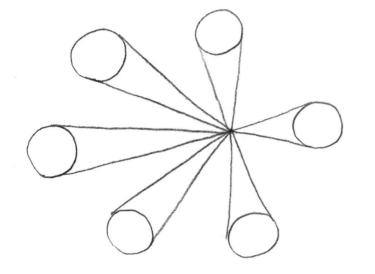

3. Using a ruler, make straight lines from the dot to the outside edges of the circles.

   Look at your drawing. Does it look like something going far away from you, or rushing toward you?

   That's the whole point of the *vanishing point.*

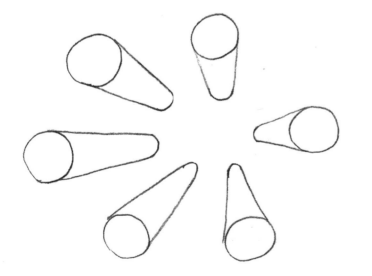

4. Now make curved lines to "chop off" the far ends. Erase the dot and straight lines close to it.

Figure out what it is you've just drawn!

Power poles on a distant asteroid?

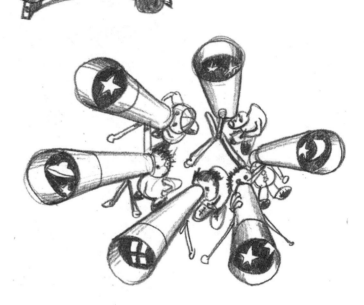

A convention of astronomers searching for power poles on a distant asteroid?

A printing press, rolling out the latest news about a convention of astronomers discovering power poles on a distant asteroid?

Or is it something else?

You decide!

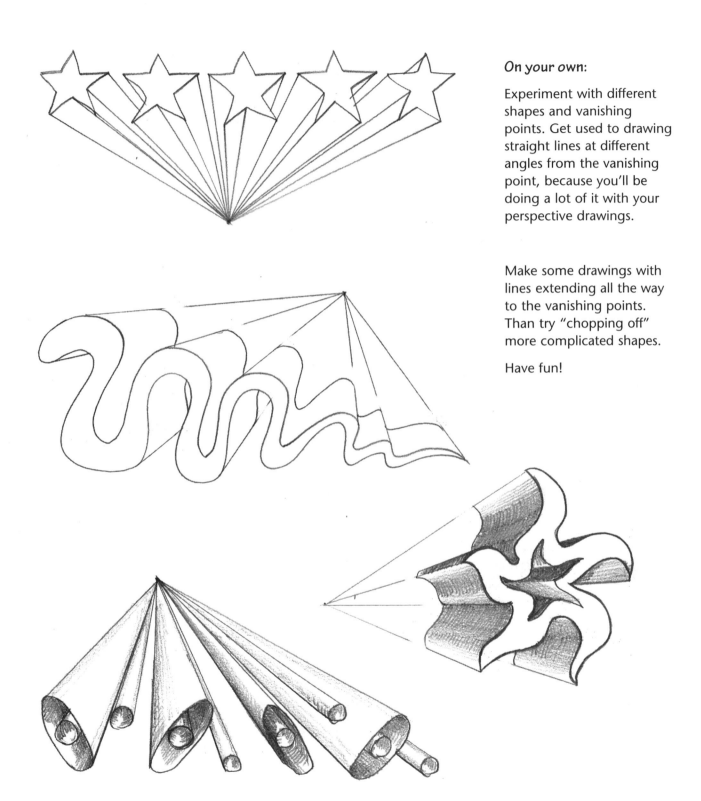

On your own:

Experiment with different shapes and vanishing points. Get used to drawing straight lines at different angles from the vanishing point, because you'll be doing a lot of it with your perspective drawings.

Make some drawings with lines extending all the way to the vanishing points. Than try "chopping off" more complicated shapes.

Have fun!

You name in 3-D

If your name is Sophronia, you can just trace this one. But, golly gee, I'll bet your name's not Sophronia. Better follow the instructions.

1. Draw a curved line. Lightly write your name on it.

2. Make the letters wider.

3. Add a vanishing point. Starting at one end, using a straightedge, make lines to connect every edge and angle with the vanishing point.

---------------------- *vanishing point*

4. Make sure you've got every line in place!

5. "Chop off" the backs of each letter by carefully copying the shape of the front.

6. Erase guide lines. *(Why is mine so neat? Because I "erased" the lines after scanning the drawing into the computer.)*

On your own:

Add shading to your letters. If your name is Sophronia, and you simply traced this, do another, using your best friend's name.

Draw a box in 3-D

1. Draw a square. Make a small dot for the *vanishing point,* and connect the three corners to it with straight <u>guide lines</u>.

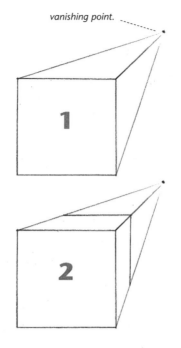

vanishing point.

1

> **Guide lines** help you set up your drawing. Usually, you'll erase them later, so draw guide lines lightly!

2. Repeat the shape of the front to make the back (one <u>horizontal</u> line, one <u>vertical</u>.)

2

> **Horizontal** lines go from side to side, like the horizon. **Vertical** lines go up and down.

3. Erase guide lines.

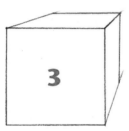

3

On your own:

Practice drawing boxes with the *vanishing point* in different directions. Also place some vanishing points closer to the box, and place some farther away.

vanishing point

Two boxes, one vanishing point

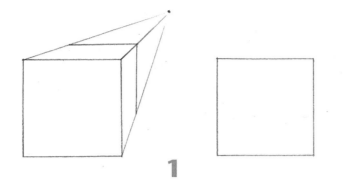

1

1. Draw a box with a vanishing point like the one on the previous page. Add another square next to it.

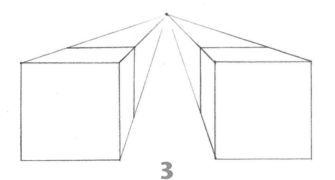

2

2. From three corners of the second square, draw straight guide lines to the vanishing point.

3

3. Add horizontal and vertical lines for the back edges of the second box.

4

4. Erase guide lines.

On your own:

1. Draw two squares with a vanishing point *directly above* one of them. Add *guide lines* and back edges.

   LOOK! *One box needs only two guide lines instead of three...and only one back edge shows.*

2. Draw two squares with a vanishing point below and between them. Add guide lines and finish.

3. Draw two squares with a vanishing point directly *below* one of them. Add guide lines and finish.

   Note: this is the same as the first drawing, only upside-down.

   The 3-D technique works the same no matter where the vanishing point lies.

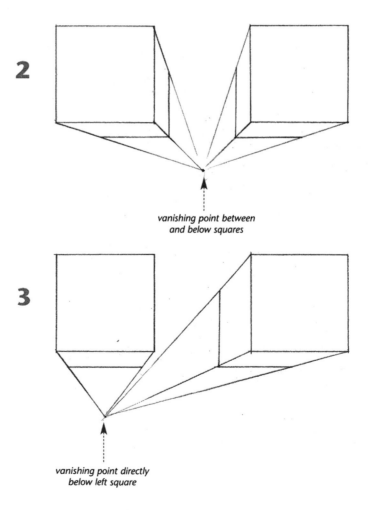

vanishing point directly above right square

1

2

vanishing point between and below squares

3

vanishing point directly below left square

Four boxes, one vanishing point

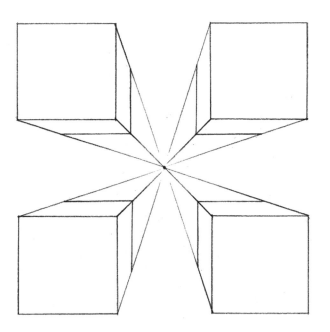

On your own:

Draw four squares with a vanishing point directly in the middle of the group.

Add guide lines and back edges.

Erase your guide lines. *(I've left mine to show you how I drew them.)*

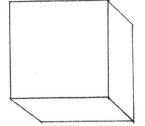 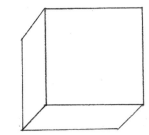

Now compare your vanishing point drawing to four boxes drawn using parallel lines to create depth. Can you see the difference?

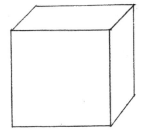 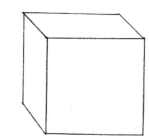

Using parallel lines to create depth, you can draw quite a few things. But if you want to create a real sense of depth in a picture, you must use a vanishing point.

More depth with a vanishing point

On your own:

Draw a box in perspective, using a vanishing point. Now add a second box behind it, using the same vanishing point guide lines. Then add another box, and another.

Notice how much smaller they get. This example really creates the feeling of a picture going into the distance.

Look at the difference between four boxes drawn to a vanishing point, and four boxes drawn with <u>parallel</u> lines. Though all four boxes are exactly the same size, the most distant one actually looks bigger, because your eye expects to see them in perspective.

Parallel *lines run in the same direction, never getting closer together or farther apart.*

Now compare the effect of simply making the more distant boxes smaller, while still drawing with parallel lines. You'll see that it doesn't quite look right, especially after looking at vanishing point drawings.

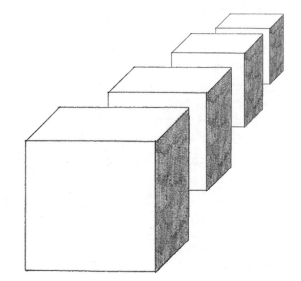

The Horizon (eye level)

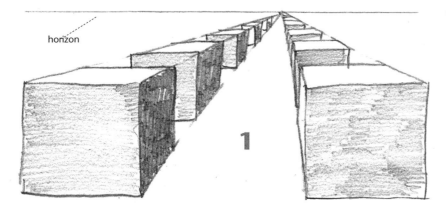

horizon

1. Perspective drawing started with buildings, which sit on the ground. If you follow the ground level for as far as you can see, you come to the horizon, where sky and earth appear to meet.

2. Even if you can't actually see it, the horizon is always there. To draw a building like the one at the left, you have to know where the horizon lies.

   If you look closely, you can see a dotted line in the drawing representing the horizon.

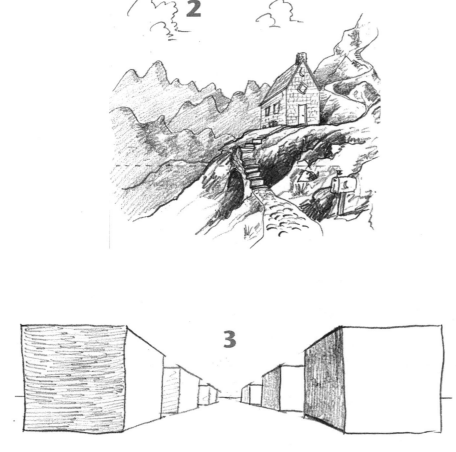

3. The horizon also represents your eye level in the drawing. If you walked up to the blocks in this drawing, where would your eye be? How much taller are the blocks than you?

On your own:

Look though magazines for pictures with buildings in them. Look for perspective at work. Locate the horizon and vanishing points.

Perspective in action: a road

vanishing point

1

1. Draw a horizontal line for the horizon near the middle of your paper. Leave plenty of room above and below it. Place a vanishing point near the center of the horizon.

2

2. From the vanishing point, draw two lines at an angle downward.

3

3. Draw two more very light lines from the vanishing point, close together in the center of the road. Divide them horizontally to make the thick dotted line running down the middle of the road.

In this photo, you can see the lines converging on a vanishing point in real life.

I wanted to take a picture of a real road, but that seemed a little dangerous. So instead of a real road, you get a railroad. The principle is the same.

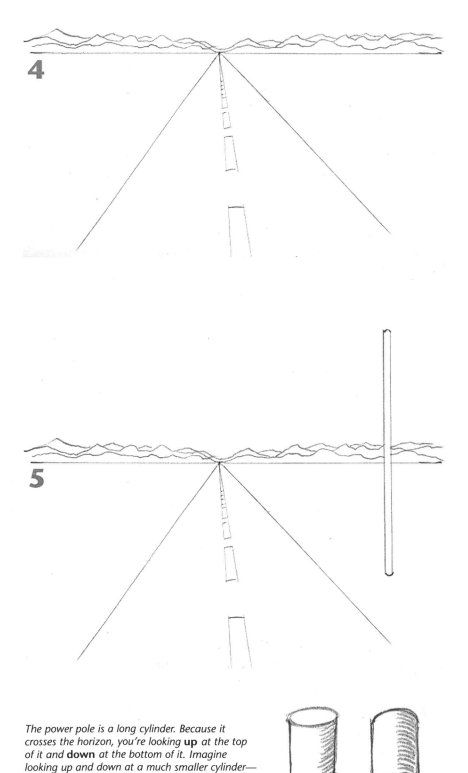

4. Since we want this to be a realistic scene, add some squiggly lines just above the horizon.

   You know they're squiggly lines. *I* know they're squiggly lines. But *someone else* looking at your drawing will think, "Ooh, look—mountains!"

5. To the right of the road, make a vertical power pole.

   Make the power pole VERTICAL. Do NOT let it lean to one side.

*The power pole is a long cylinder. Because it crosses the horizon, you're looking **up** at the top of it and **down** at the bottom of it. Imagine looking up and down at a much smaller cylinder—can you see why both the top and bottom of the power pole are rounded?*

6. From the power pole
(which you drew vertically,
not leaning to one side),
draw two light <u>guide lines</u>
to the vanishing point.

6

> **Guide lines** *help you set up your drawing. Usually, you'll want to erase them later, so draw your guide lines lightly!*

7. Add a second power pole,
extending from one guide
line to the other. Place it
about halfway from the first
power pole to the vanishing
point.

Make the power pole VERTICAL, and thinner. Do NOT let it lean to one side.

7

> **Vertical** *lines go up and down. In this drawing, your brain will want to make the power poles lean. Don't let it!*

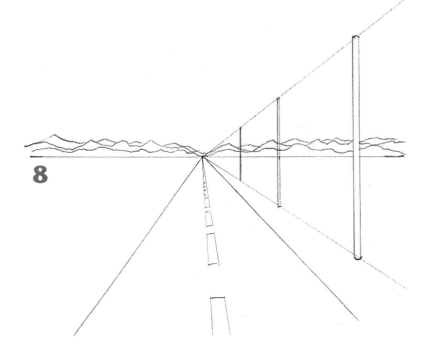

8. Add another power pole, from one guide line to the other, about halfway between the second power pole and the vanishing point.

   Make the power pole thinner, and VERTICAL. *Do* NOT *let it lean to one side.*

   Make the power pole VERTICAL. *Do* NOT *let it lean to one side.*

   Make the power pole VERTICAL.

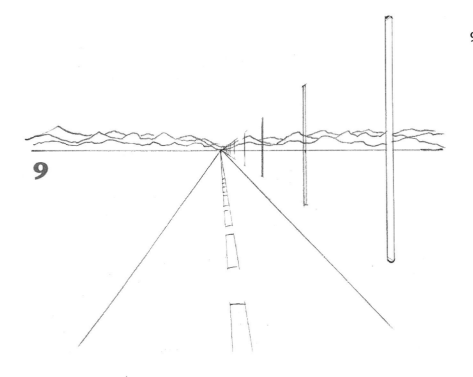

9. Keep adding power poles until you can't add any more!

   Then erase your guide lines.

TIME OUT!

So far, this drawing may be going perfectly smoothly for you. Still, pause a moment to compare these examples with your drawing *just in case....*

a. Power poles are leaning. If yours are, it's best to start again. Look carefully at the side of your paper as you draw. Or use a drawing tool such as a triangle. Or perhaps draw on a piece of notebook paper turned sideways, so the little blue lines run vertically.

b. Power poles all the same thickness. The power poles get shorter farther away— and they also get thinner.

c. Power poles evenly spaced. In creating the illusion of depth in your drawing, you have to watch every detail: the smaller power poles also appear to be closer together as they go into the distance.

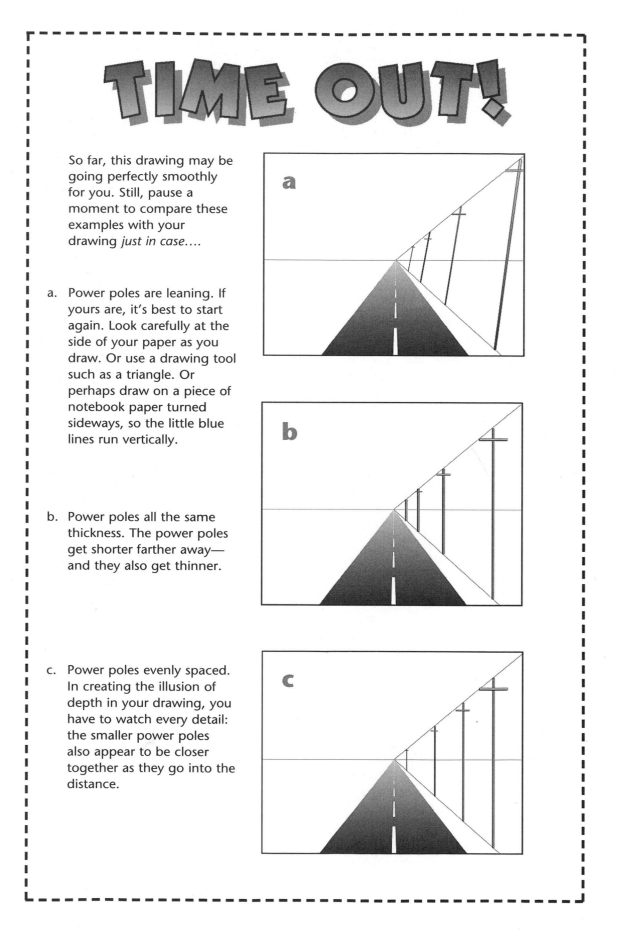

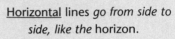
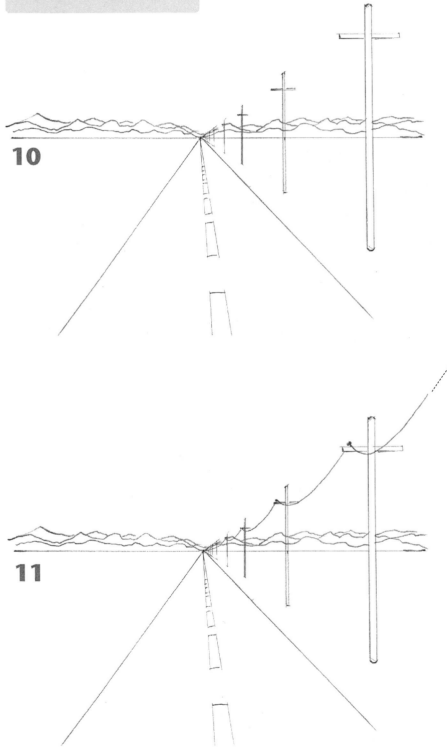

10. Draw short horizontal cross arms to carry the wires on each pole.

11. On the left side of each cross arm, make a little spot for the insulator, which keeps the wire from short-circuiting on the wood or metal pole.

   From one insulator to another, make a swooping line.

   From the pole closest to you, continue the line to the edge of the picture.

12. Add the other wire. Draw it going behind the poles.

12

13. On the left side of the road, draw a short vertical fence post. From the top and bottom, draw light guide lines to the vanishing point.

13

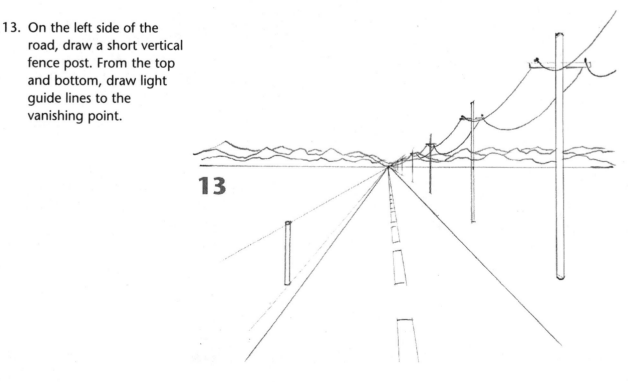

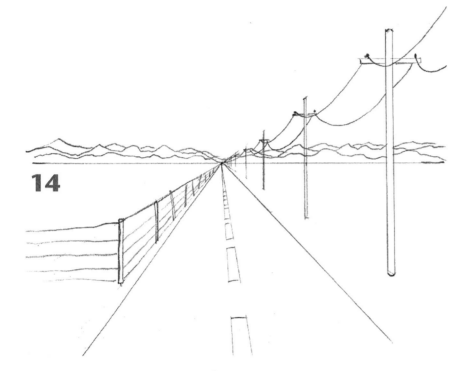

14. Add more fence posts, between the top and the bottom guide line, getting smaller and closer together as they go into the distance. (It's OK if they lean a little, because fences are like that.)

Add lines for wires, converging on the vanishing point.

Draw lines straight out to the side to make the fence turn away from the road. They should be horizontal.

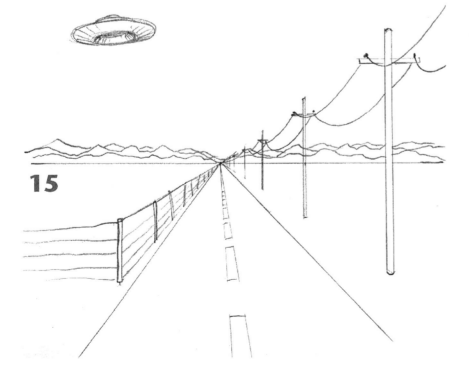

15. From a distant asteroid, a mysterious craft has arrived to inspect power poles. Draw the craft.

16. From the sides of the mysterious craft, draw two light guide lines to the vanishing point. Add the second craft, inside the guide lines.

Keep it horizontal—don't make it tilting over to the side!

Hint: try making a light, horizontal line as a guide before drawing the ellipse of the second mysterious craft.

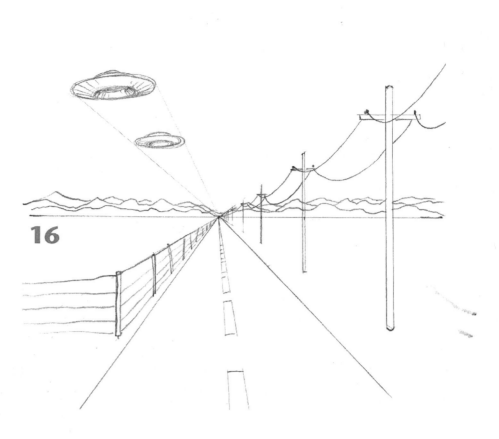

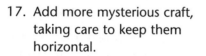

17. Add more mysterious craft, taking care to keep them horizontal.

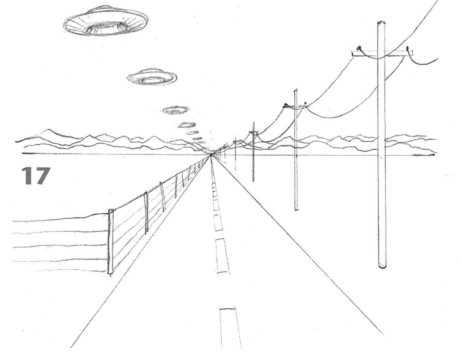

18. You can use several "tricks" to make your drawing look more real. Because of the atmosphere, more distant objects have less contrast.

   In other words, the dark road gets lighter in the distance, while the white ground gets slightly grey.

   Add hazy shadows, and a few curly marks in the sky. They may end up looking like clouds if you do them right!

19. Add realistic details to make your drawing more believable. Using your knowledge of 3-D drawing, add a moving truck, carrying telescopes to a far-off mountain where a convention of astronomers search for power poles on distant asteroids. Create some giant mutant arachnids, which must have something to do with those mysterious craft...

   ...*anything to make the drawing more believable.*

Perspective in action: an interior

Perspective works inside as well as outside. Try drawing this interior view, using a vanishing point to create depth.

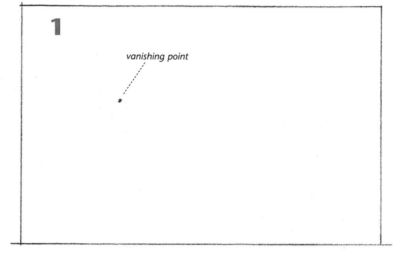

1. Draw a large rectangle. Place the vanishing point off-center.

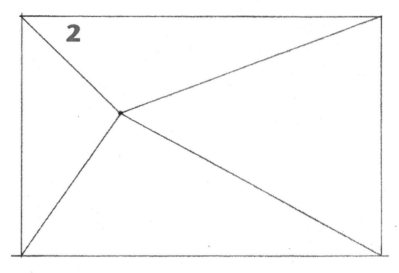

2. Draw straight lines connecting each corner to the vanishing point.

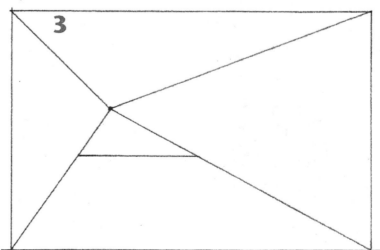

3. Draw a horizontal line to make the bottom of the back wall.

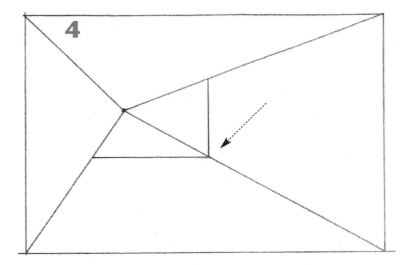

4. Where the bottom of the wall intersects the line from the vanishing point, draw a vertical line for the side of the wall.

5. Make another horizontal line for the top of the wall.

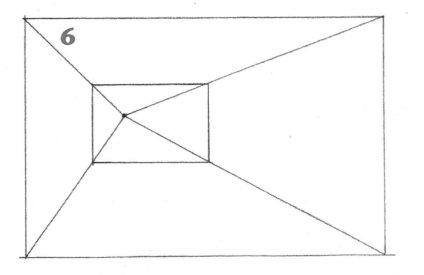

6. Complete the back wall by drawing another vertical line.

7. From the vanishing point, draw two more guide lines along the right side wall.

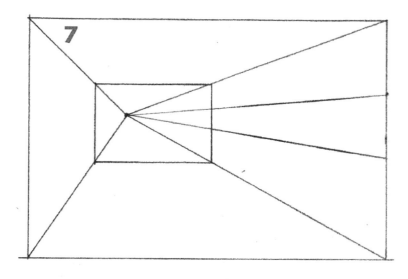

8. Before going further, erase all the lines inside the area of the back wall. But don't erase the vanishing point. You still need it!

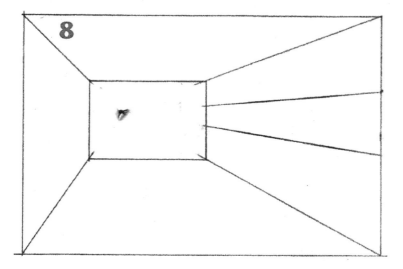

9. Where the two guide lines intersect the back wall, make two horizontal lines across the back wall.

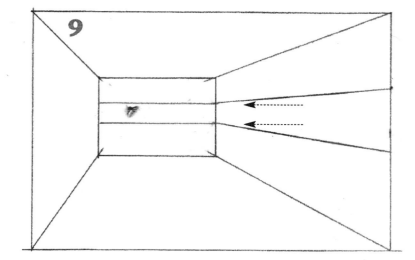

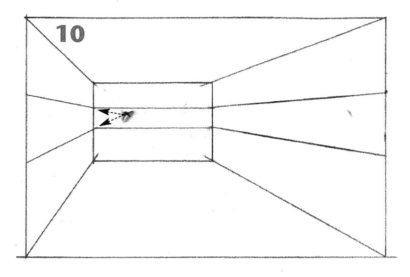

10. Draw two more guide lines where the horizontal lines intersect the side wall.

11. Draw vertical lines for doors on the right side of the hallway. Make the closer door wider than the one farther away.

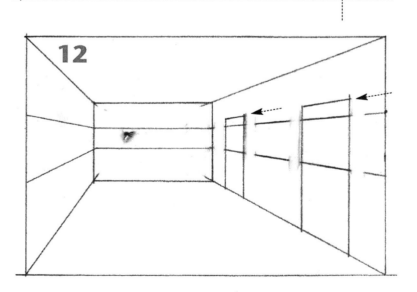

12. Draw lines for the tops of the doors. Erase guide lines next to the doors.

13. Draw two horizontal guide lines from the bottom corners of the doors. These allow you to place two doors in the same position across the hall.

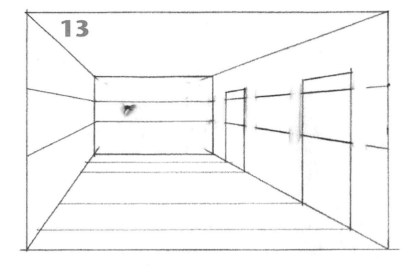

14. From those guide lines, draw vertical lines for the sides of the two doors.

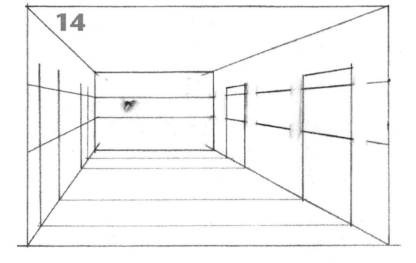

15. Line up your ruler on the vanishing point, then add the tops of the doors on the left side.

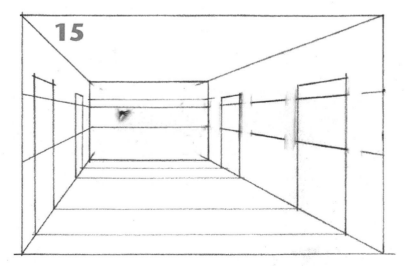

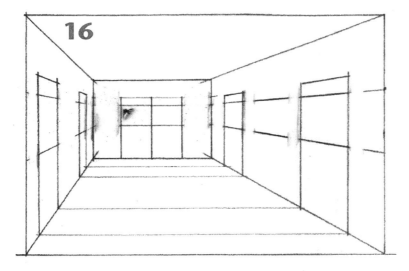

16. Draw the doors on the back wall.

17. Draw as many details as you can to create the feeling of depth...try drawing lights overhead, a carpet on the floor, and a bulletin board on the wall.

18. Add shading and details to complete your drawing. Of course you can add people to your drawing as well— just make sure they appear smaller farther away!

Dividing spaces evenly

In the preceding drawing, a question naturally arises: how do you know what size to make objects in perspective? Your best guide is your eye. Draw it the way it looks best.

If you want to divide an area more precisely, here's a technique you can use.

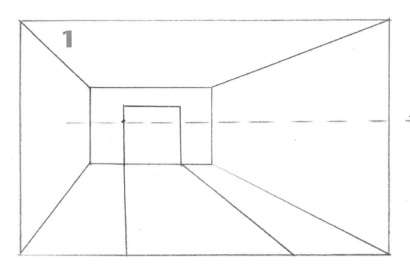

1. Draw the horizon (even if you can't see it in the picture), and make a vanishing point off to the side.

2. From this vanishing point, draw a guide line to intersect what you're dividing—in this case, the carpet.

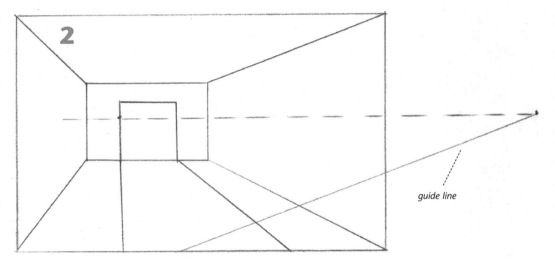

3. Where the guide line intersects the edge of the carpet, draw a horizontal line across the carpet.

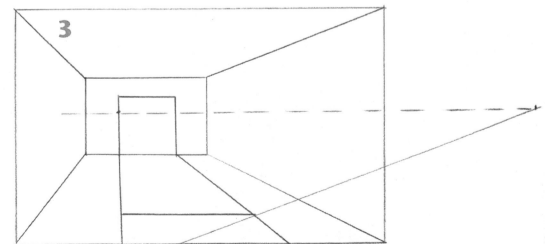

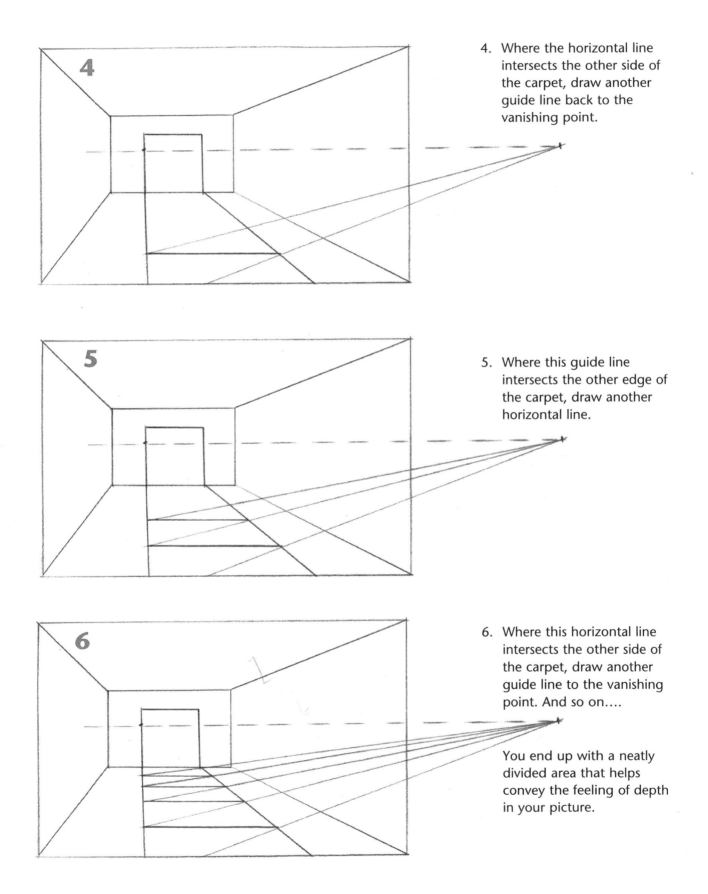

4. Where the horizontal line intersects the other side of the carpet, draw another guide line back to the vanishing point.

5. Where this guide line intersects the other edge of the carpet, draw another horizontal line.

6. Where this horizontal line intersects the other side of the carpet, draw another guide line to the vanishing point. And so on....

You end up with a neatly divided area that helps convey the feeling of depth in your picture.

A bridge

Reflections can make an impressive addition to your drawing. Try them!

1. Draw the shape you see.

2. Add stair steps on both sides. (Notice that you've already drawn a reflection of sorts—the two sides mirror each other.)

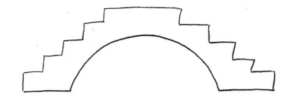

vanishing point

3. Draw the horizon and a vanishing point above the steps. Using a ruler, draw guide lines from each angle of the bridge back toward the vanishing point.

   Note: you don't need to draw the guide lines all the way to the vanishing point.

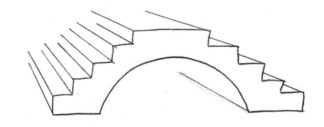

4. Add some shading underneath the bridge.

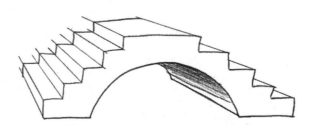

5. Draw the sides of a stream meandering from the horizon, and running under the bridge.

   Take your time drawing this—it's not so easy to make it look good!

6. Add mountains in the background, some shading along the stream, a couple of fish playing in it, and...oh yes...a reflection of the bridge in the water!

   Hint: if you have trouble figuring this out, try imagining the land and water reflecting, as though the entire bridge were sitting on a mirror. Draw the whole bridge, then erase the parts on the land. To make it even easier, turn your paper upside down....

7. Can you figure out how to draw this? Give it a try!

   If not, don't worry: after all, it's highly unlikely that someone would put a mirror at the end of a bridge, so why would you want to draw one there anyway? Because it's a great drawing exercise!

Two-point perspective

A box drawn with a single vanishing point has limitations. Adding a second vanishing point opens up new possibilities.

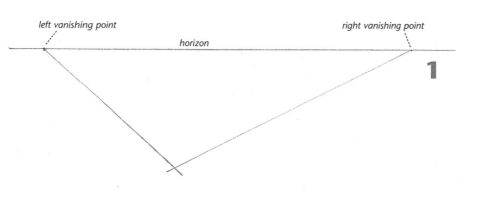

1. Draw a horizon, and two widely spaced vanishing points. From the vanishing points, draw lines downward until they intersect.

2. Draw a second line from each vanishing point, to create the base of a box.

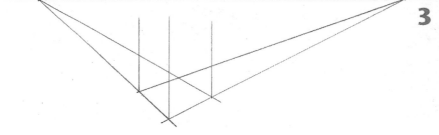

3. From the three closest corners of the base, draw vertical lines for the edges of the box.

4. Decide where the top of the box will be, by marking the closest vertical line.

   From that point, extend lines toward the two vanishing points to create the top edges of the box.

   You don't have to draw the lines all the way to the vanishing point—just far enough to complete the top of the box!

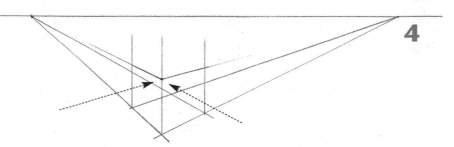

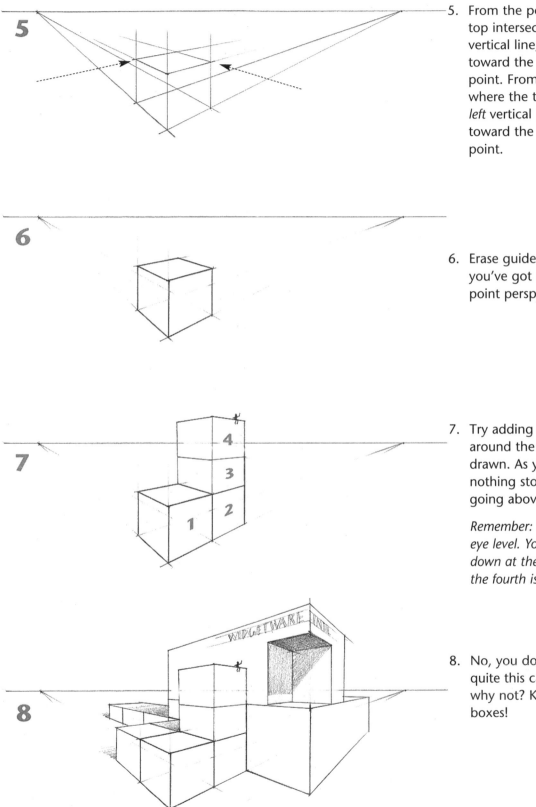

5. From the point where the top intersects the *right* vertical line, draw a line toward the *left* vanishing point. From the point where the top intersects the *left* vertical line, draw a line toward the *right* vanishing point.

6. Erase guide lines, and you've got a box in two-point perspective!

7. Try adding more boxes around the one you've drawn. As you can see, nothing stops you from going above the horizon.

   Remember: horizon is your eye level. You're looking down at the first three boxes; the fourth is at eye level.

8. No, you don't have to get quite this carried away...but why not? Keep adding boxes!

A ramp

Drawing a sloping surface in perspective follows the same principles as drawing a box. It's all logical—just a little more confusing.

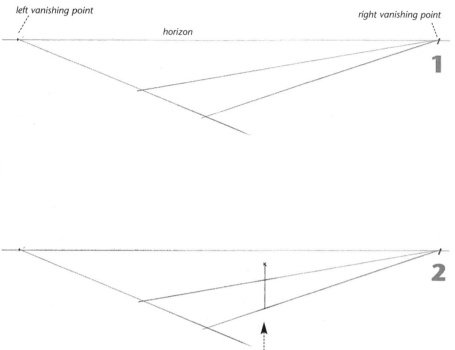

1. Draw a horizon with two widely spaced vanishing points. Draw one line from the left vanishing point, and two lines from the right vanishing point.

2. Pick a point for the end of the ramp, and from there draw a vertical line.

3. From the closest corner, draw a line to the top of the ramp.

4. From the top of your ramp, draw a line to the left vanishing point.

left vanishing point   *horizon*   *right vanishing point*

1

2

3

left vanishing point

4

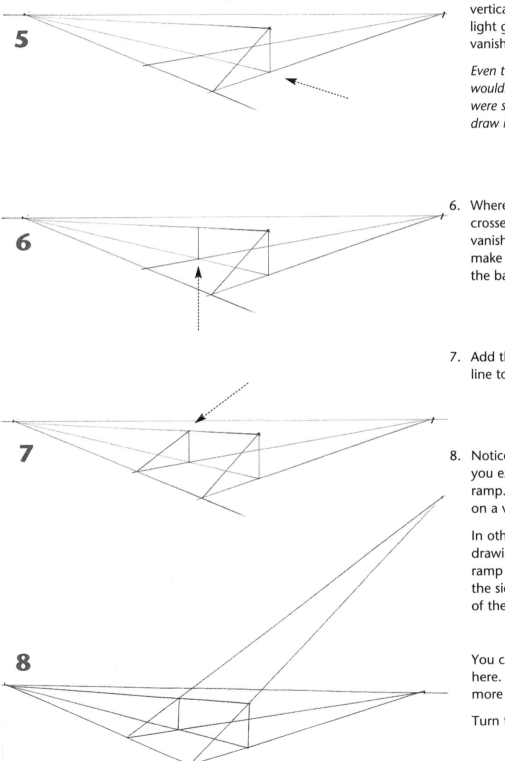

5. At the bottom of the vertical line, draw a very light guide line to the left vanishing point.

   Even though this line wouldn't show if the ramp were solid, you still have to draw it...can you see why?

6. Where this guide line crosses the next right vanishing point guide line, make a vertical line. This is the back edge.

7. Add the remaining sloping line to complete the ramp.

8. Notice what happens when you extend the sides of the ramp. They, too, converge on a vanishing point.

   In other words, in this drawing, the sides of the ramp aren't parallel, just as the sides, top and bottom of the box aren't parallel.

   You can stop your drawing here. Or you can make it more complicated

   Turn the page...

For experts only!

1. Draw another vertical line (arrow), and use the left vanishing point to draw another rectangle in perspective.

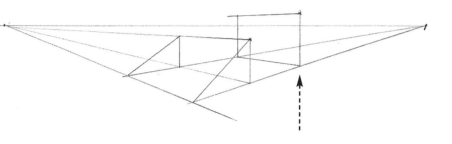

2. Draw another rectangle— find the top by putting your ruler on the right vanishing point and the top of the ramp (arrows). This way, it's the same height as the ramp.

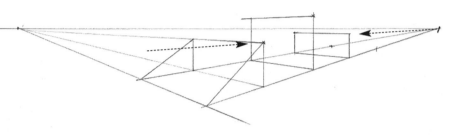

3. Draw diagonal lines to connect the ramp and the taller rectangle.

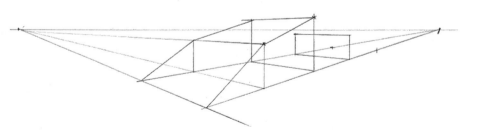

4. Draw diagonal lines to connect the last rectangle.

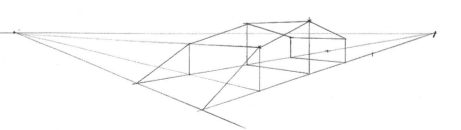

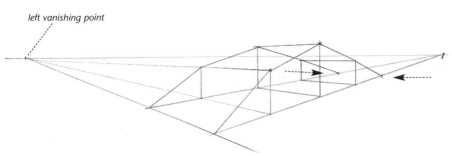

5. Draw the two last diagonal lines. Use your ruler and the left vanishing point to make sure the ends are in perspective.

6. From the closer edge of this bridge-like structure, make two vertical lines downward.

7. If you've made it this far, I think you're in a good position to keep exploring on your own. Follow my example, or go wild and invent your own structure.

   It can go up, it can go sideways...it just has to stay between the two vanishing points.

   Which is something we should talk about next....

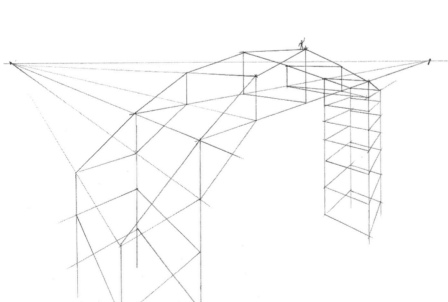

Vanishing points...

You can create different feelings in your picture depending on where you place the vanishing points.

1. Placing them close together, as we've done for convenience so far, creates the sense of objects looming toward you—rather dramatic.

2. A more "normal" view might not have *any* vanishing points in the picture—maybe one, but certainly not two.

3. The farther the vanishing points lie to the side, the less apparent distortion your viewer will see in the finished drawing.

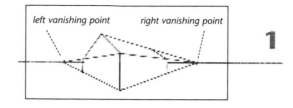

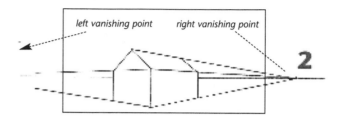

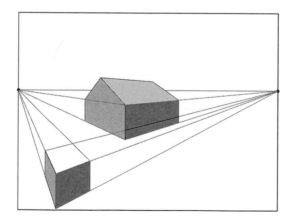

You might find it difficult to draw vanishing points off the side of your paper, unless you have a drafting table, but...

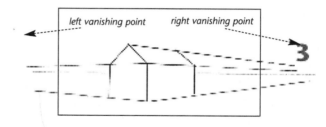

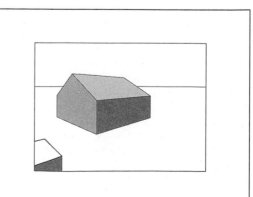

...by cropping the picture, you get the same effect.

...and camera lenses

If you've ever used a camera with a zoom lens, you will see a connection.

1. Vanishing points in the picture, or close to the edge of the picture, create a wide-angle view.

2. Vanishing points farther out create a "normal" view.

3. When the vanishing points lie far outside the picture, lines converging on them look almost parallel. This creates the effect of a telephoto lens.

   (Look at the wonderful perspective in the lawn!)

Here's another example of a different camera lens (actually a zoom lens, using different focal lengths).

Can you locate the vanishing points for the truck in these two photos?

More about the horizon...

Here's are some real examples of changing horizon and eye level.

1. Perched on the scorching hot fender of another school bus (this was a used school bus lot), I was looking *down* at this school bus, so it lies *below* the horizon in the picture.

   Can you find the horizon is in this photo?

2. Back on the ground *(phew!)* I take another photo. Where's the horizon? Where's my eye level?

   (How tall am I?)

3. Now the bus looms above me *(look familiar?)*. Look at the lines on the side of the bus. Where's the horizon? Where is their vanishing point?

   Look at the lines on the grille on the front of the bus—where's their vanishing point?

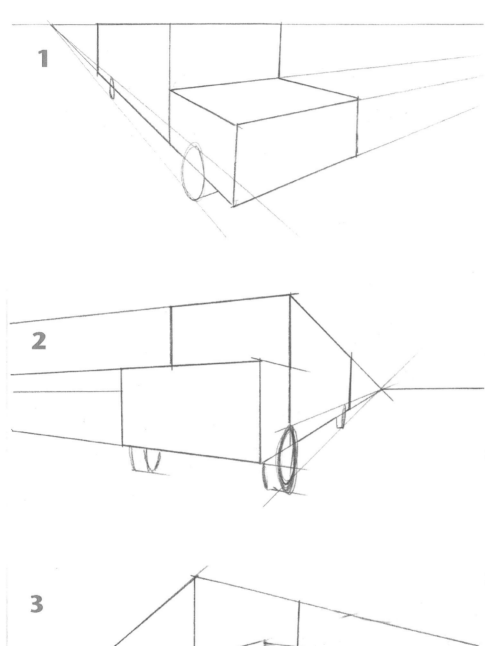

Look at the photographs on the opposite page. I'll bet they look perfectly normal, right? Now try drawing rough box drawings of each. You will be amazed how *weird* they are!

Try drawing them freehand (without a ruler) if you want. In reality, things like school buses aren't perfect boxes, so drawings like these would be just the starting point of a real drawing. Imagine these clunky boxes as bars of soap, which you would then carve to make the final drawing, once the correct perspective is established.

1. How strange—the horizon lies exactly at the top of the bus. Look at the photo—it really does. Draw it.

2. From this angle, the rear wheel becomes surprisingly small compared to the front. Just follow the rules, and draw it.

3. Same here—can the rear wheel really be that small? Measure it on the photo. Look at the guidelines. Follow the rules of 3-D.

    Just draw it.

Curved objects in 3-D

Not every vehicle has the convenient boxy look of a school bus. But the same principles of perspective apply.

1. Draw a box outline similar to the school bus.

2. Add wheels, using the vanishing point and guidelines to keep them in perspective with each other.

   Note that the ellipse for the front wheel is slightly wider than the rear wheel, making the front wheel appear slightly turned.

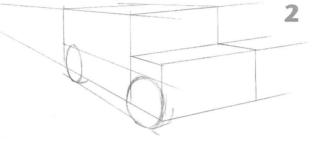

3. Add a curved fender, going behind the back of the front wheel, and covering part of the front. Continue the curve across the bottom of the car's front, and make the opposite fender.

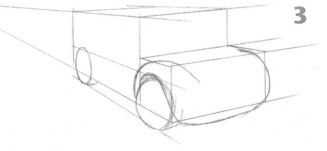

4. Draw the rear fender and line along the bottom of the side.

5. Add the curving top of the car, and the outline of the windows on the side.

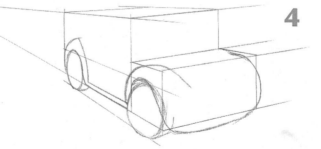

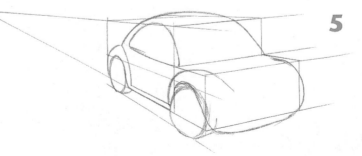

6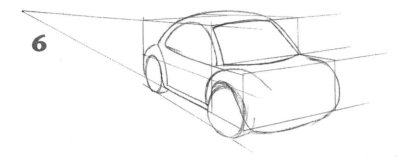

6. Draw the windshield. Notice how the top curves up, and the bottom curves down.

7

7. Add ovals for headlights, one wider and one thinner.

8

8. Draw details: lines for the door, rear view mirrors, hood insignia, parking lights, wheel details....

9. Erase guide lines, add some shading, and presto! It's a car in perspective!

If you're interested in drawing cars, see page 64 for information about ordering Draw Cars.

A 3-D checkerboard

The beauty of perspective, or 3-D drawing is the wonderful effects of depth you can achieve. The downside is the drudgery of drawing *all those lines.* As you complete this drawing, you'll see what I mean.

1. Draw a horizon, two vanishing points (VP1, VP2), and two sets of guide lines.

2. From the closer to the farther intersections of the two sets of lines, make a new guide line to the horizon to establish a new vanishing point (VP3).

3. From VP3, draw a line to...well, look at the drawing.

4. This new guide line creates yet another intersection. From it, draw a line back to VP1.

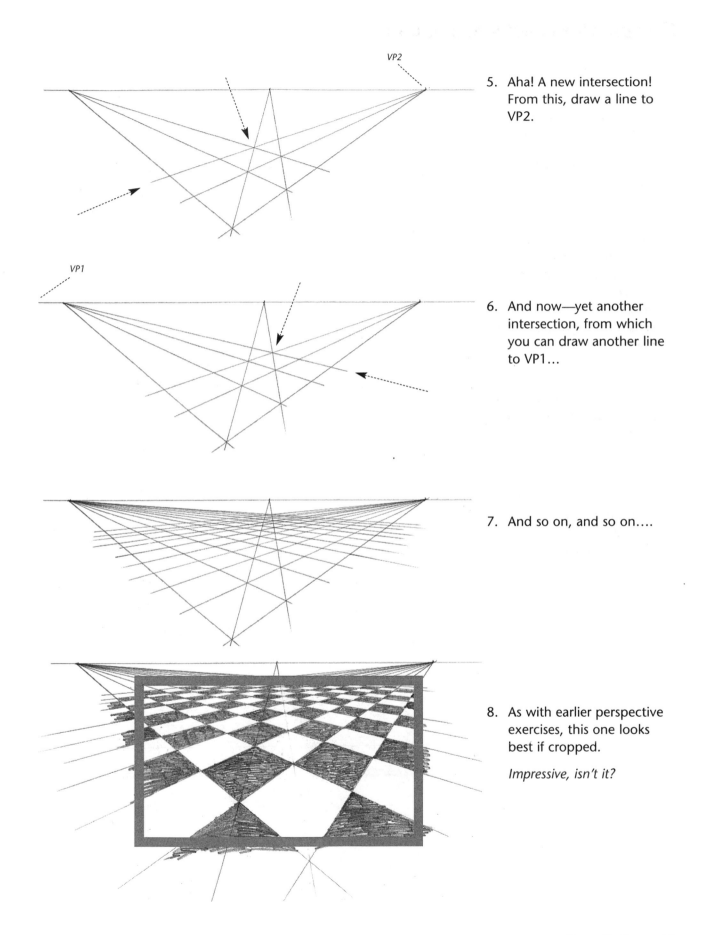

5. Aha! A new intersection! From this, draw a line to VP2.

6. And now—yet another intersection, from which you can draw another line to VP1...

7. And so on, and so on....

8. As with earlier perspective exercises, this one looks best if cropped.

   Impressive, isn't it?

Perspective in action: a house

For convenience in this picture, I've placed the vanishing points close together. A more "normal" view would position the vanishing points well outside the picture.

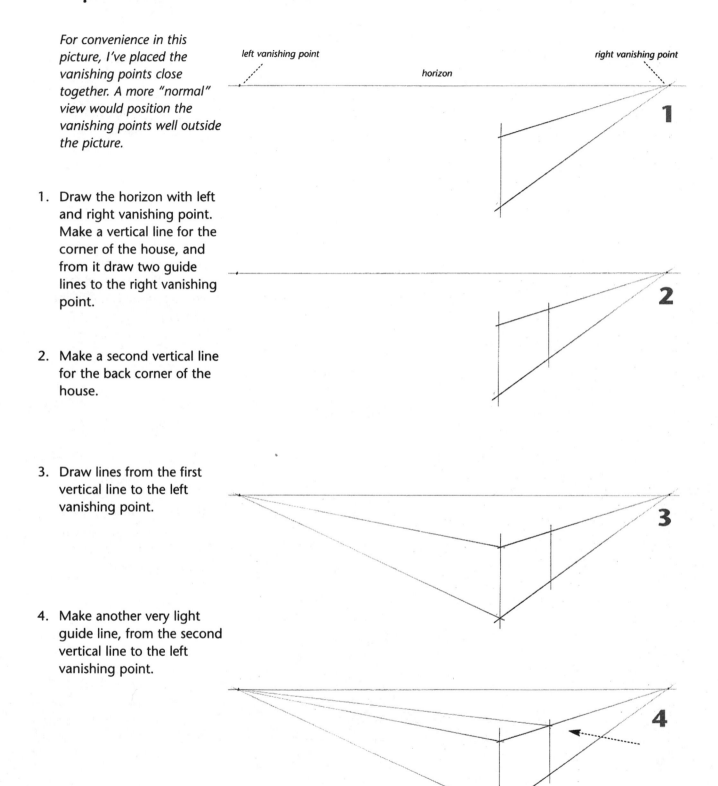

1. Draw the horizon with left and right vanishing point. Make a vertical line for the corner of the house, and from it draw two guide lines to the right vanishing point.

2. Make a second vertical line for the back corner of the house.

3. Draw lines from the first vertical line to the left vanishing point.

4. Make another very light guide line, from the second vertical line to the left vanishing point.

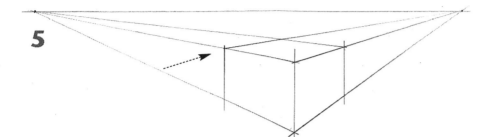

5. Draw a vertical line for the third corner of the house. Make another very light guide line to the right vanishing point.

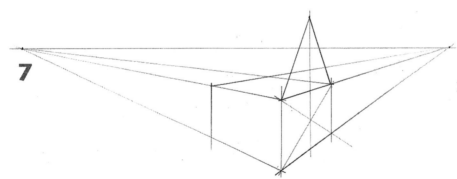

6. To put the peak of the roof over the center of the wall, we have to find the center of the wall. Do this with light lines connecting the corners.

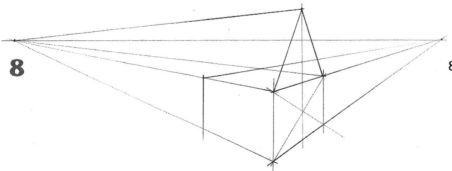

7. From the center of the X on the wall, make a vertical line. From the top of it, draw the sloping lines of the roof.

8. From the peak of the roof, make a guide line to the left vanishing point.

9. Now we need to locate the other end of the roof.

   From the center of the top of the right wall (where the vertical line to the roof peak crosses), draw a light guide line to locate the center of the back wall.

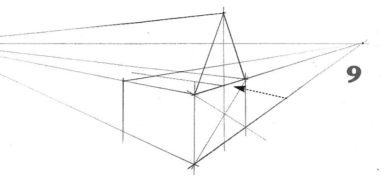

9

10. From the center of the back wall, draw a vertical line. The back end of the roof is where it crosses the top guide line.

10

11. Draw the sloping line for the back of the roof.

11

12. Let's make an addition!

   Draw two lines from the left vanishing point to extend the wall of the house.

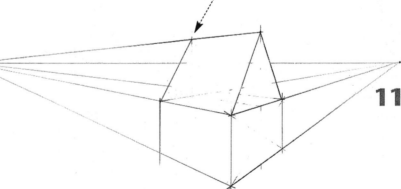

12

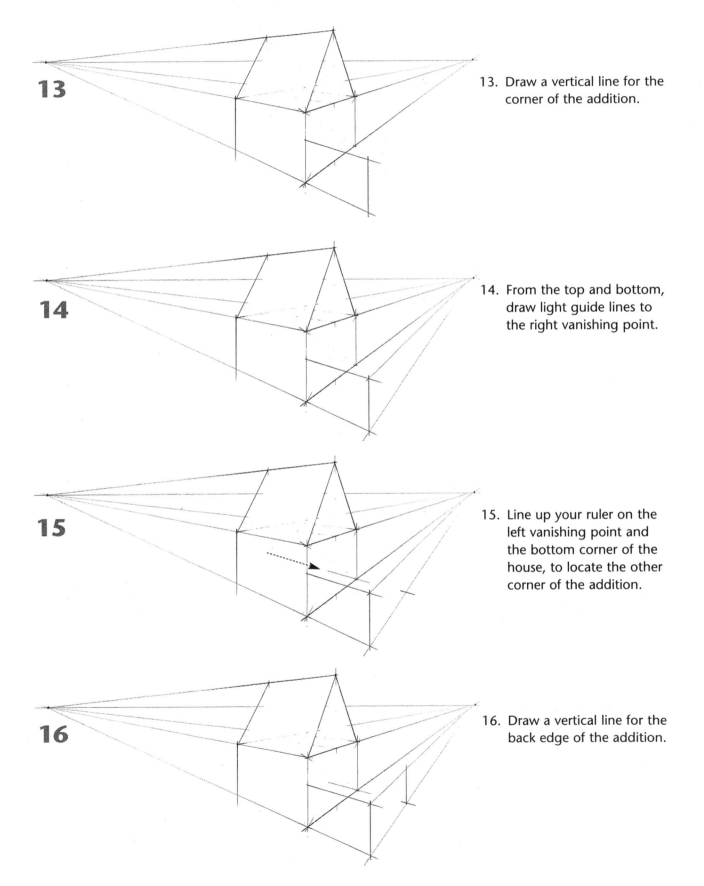

13. Draw a vertical line for the corner of the addition.

14. From the top and bottom, draw light guide lines to the right vanishing point.

15. Line up your ruler on the left vanishing point and the bottom corner of the house, to locate the other corner of the addition.

16. Draw a vertical line for the back edge of the addition.

17. From that line, draw one sloping line to the house...

18. ...and another.

19. Add details to the house and its surroundings. Draw some barns with different roof angles. Add a swimming pool, some fields, and roads.

Draw a light grid of guide lines in the sky, and follow it as you draw clouds. Even though irregular in shape, clouds can add perspective to your drawing as well.

Hey! What's this I see? Better draw some power poles, too, because I see a power pole inspection craft approaching....

light source

Adding shadows in 3-D

Shadows in perspective drawing also use vanishing points—but not always in obvious ways.

shadow vanishing point

1

Light source behind

1. Draw a basic house using two-point perspective. Leave room at the top for the light source, and room at the bottom for the shadow.

   Mark the light source on your paper, and *directly beneath it* on the horizon, mark the *shadow vanishing point*.

2

2. From the shadow vanishing point, draw lines through the outside corners of the house, at ground level.

3

3. Draw another line from the shadow vanishing point through the closest corner of the house, at ground level.

4

4. Draw another line from the shadow vanishing point through the middle of the end wall, at ground level.

light source

5. Now, from the *light source,* draw a line through the corner of the house directly above the first shadow vanishing point line you drew. *You don't have to draw the entire line: you're simply looking for the point at which it intersects the line from the shadow vanishing point (arrow).*

5

6. From the light source, draw another line through the closest corner of the roof until it meets the second line from the shadow vanishing point.

   Make a line connecting this point with the point established in step 5.

6

7. From the light source, draw a line through the peak of the roof until it reaches the shadow vanishing point line running through the center of the house.

   Make a line connecting this point with the point established in step 6.

7

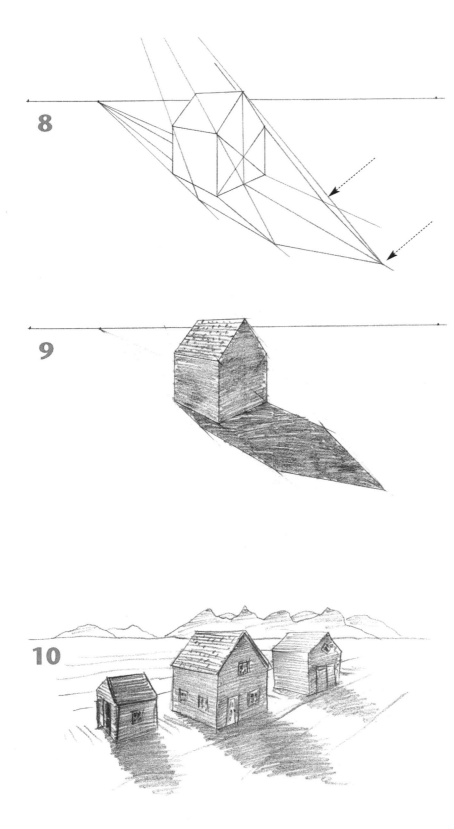

8

9

10

8. From the light source, draw a line through the far corner of the roof until it intersects the farthest line from the shadow vanishing point.

   This one is a little tricky— remember, follow the rules!

9. Erase guidelines and shade in shadow areas, and now you have a very precise shadow of the house.

   The questions is, do you need a very precise shadow of the house?

   Not really.

   However, by practicing a few shadows using technical perspective drawing, you'll understand how they work, and it will be easier to "fake" them in drawings…

   …because nobody (except for fellow artists) actually looks at the shadows in a drawing or painting.

10. Once your eye becomes atuned to shadows and perspective, you'll simply see them and draw them.

   And nobody will question whether they're real!

More shadows in 3-D

Light source in front

When the light source casts a shadow behind objects, you need a light vanishing point rather than a light source—beneath the horizon!

1. Draw a house in two-point perspective. Between the house vanishing points on the horizon, make the shadow vanishing point. Directly below it, make the light vanishing point.

2. From the shadow vanishing point, draw a line to the left corner of the house.

3. Now add a line to the point on the ground directly below the peak of the roof.

4. Draw another line to the next corner of the house.

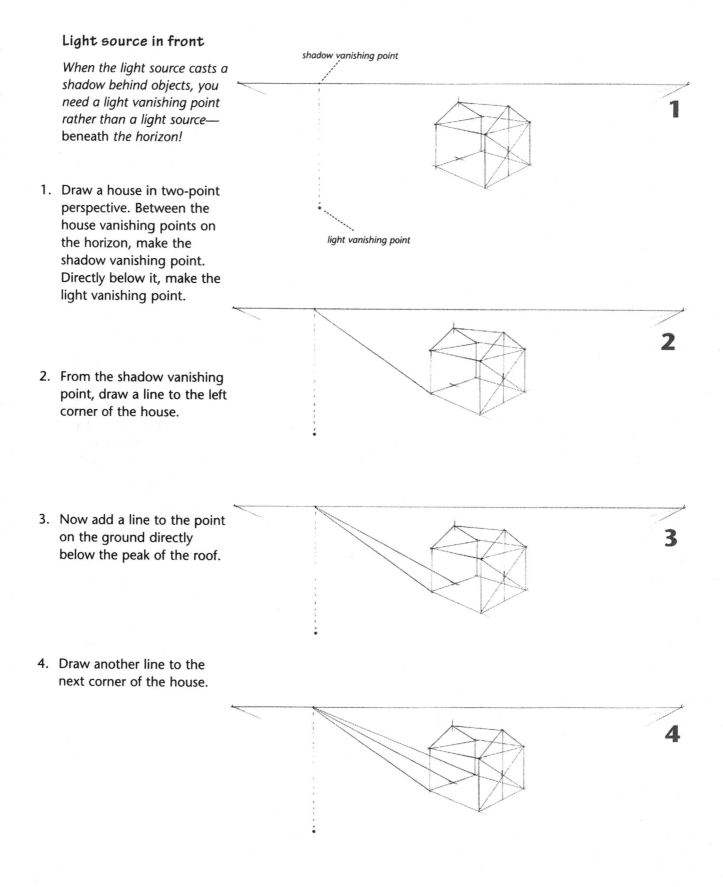

shadow vanishing point

light vanishing point

1

2

3

4

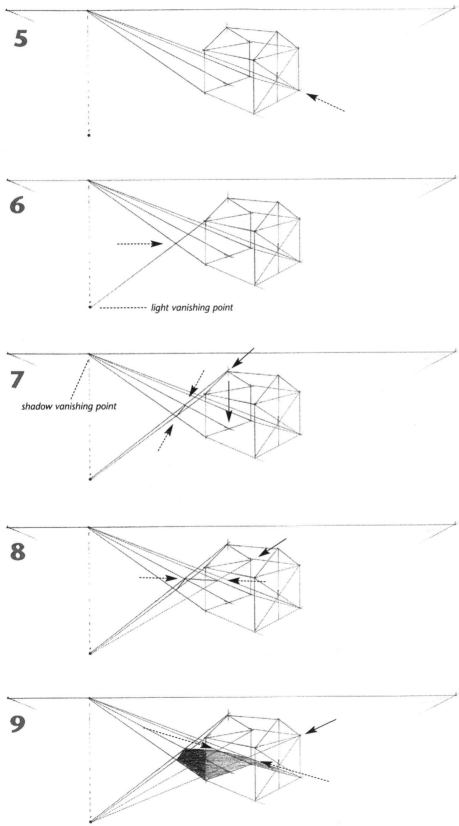

5. The shadow vanishing point can still "see" one more corner of the house. Draw a line to it.

6. From the light vanishing point, draw a line to the corner of the roof directly above the first shadow vanishing point line. Notice where the two lines intersect.

7. Also from the light vanishing point, draw a line to the peak of the roof. Follow the line lying directly beneath the peak of the roof, toward the shadow vanishing point. Where the two lines intersect, draw a line connecting them with the intersection you created in the last step.

8. Draw a line to the next corner of the roof, and repeat step 7.

9. Do it once again for the third corner of the roof.

   You now have established a precise shadow for the house, but notice, after all that work, how much of the shadow is hidden. (After all, it *is* behind the house.)

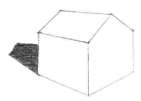

3-point perspective

You can add a third vanishing point for even more dramatic effects.

1

1. Draw two rectangles in two-point perspective.

2. Now add a third vanishing point, *very far* off the bottom edge of your paper paper.

    Draw lines from all the corners to your third vanishing point.

    Pretty cool!

    On pages 32-33, I show a way to divide receding spaces evenly using a vanishing point. Here's an even easier way to do it.

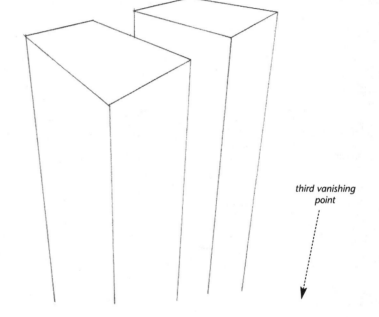

2

third vanishing
point

3. From your first two vanishing points, draw lines to establish the top floor of the buildings.

    In the middle of one of them, connect the corners to make an X. From the center of the X, draw a line to your third vanishing point—but only until it crosses the line you just drew.

    Now you have the center of the bottom of this floor.

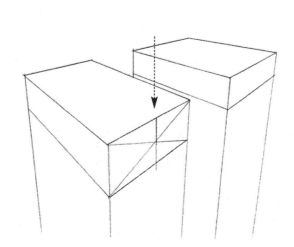

3

Another way to divide space

4

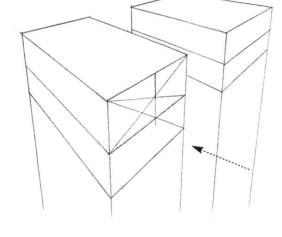

4. From the top corner of the top floor, draw a light line through the center of the bottom.

   Where it intersects with the side of the building, make a very light mark and use this to create the next floor.

5

5. Repeat the procedure. Once you understand the concept, you can simply make light marks as you go, rather than drawing lots of diagonal lines you don't want in the final drawing.

6

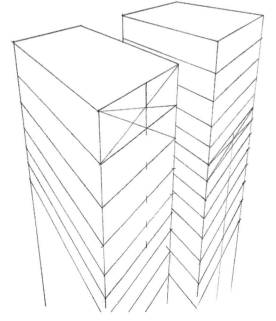

6. When you can no longer divide the floors on the closer building, you can pick up on the farther building, making an X and continuing.

4-point perspective?

You can see that a third vanishing point also works when you look up.

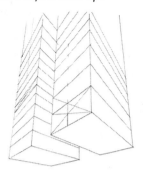

If you look straight ahead, would you then use four vanishing points?

1. No. But...

2. ...if you allow the lines to curve, as with a fisheye lens, it works. This is actually what your eye sees. Your brain makes straight lines.

The laser paradox

3. Imagine standing outside one night, and seeing an unbending laser beam, shining over your head.

4. You turn the other direction, and there's the same beam, now shining at a different angle!

5. You know the beam doesn't bend—how does it connect in the middle? Take a deep breath, let your mind go blank—and sure enough, you'll see the beam as your eye does: a curve.

    You don't need a laser. Try it facing the wall of a large room, like a gym.

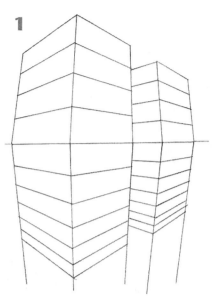

1

2

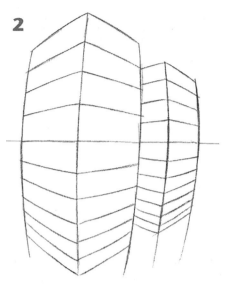

3

4

5

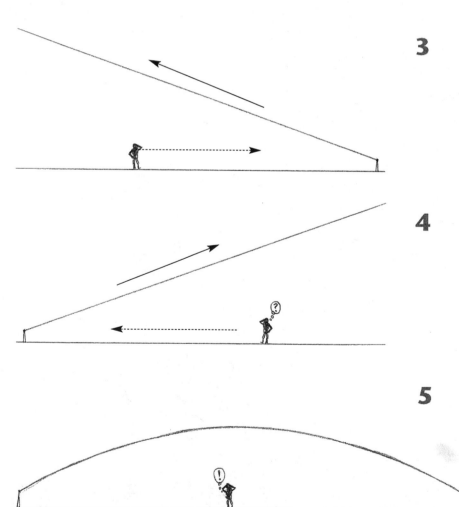

Multiple vanishing points

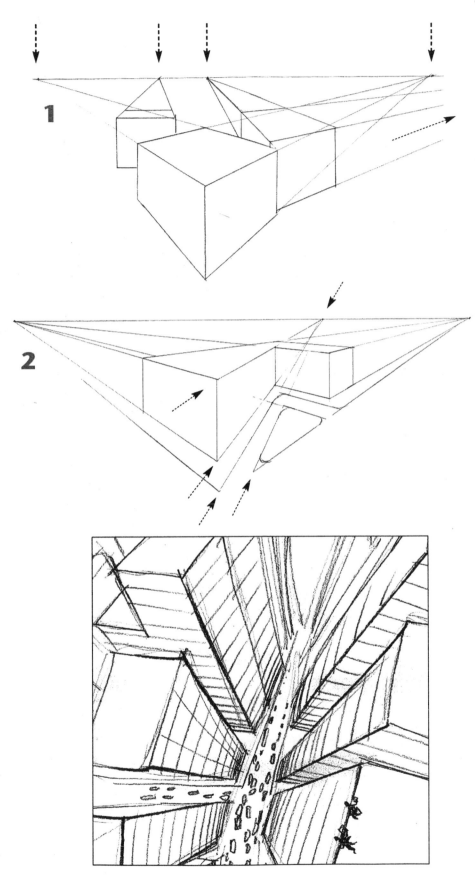

While four-point perspective doesn't really work, that doesn't mean your drawing is limited to two or three vanishing points.

1. If the objects you're drawing are not aligned with each other (parallel), then naturally each will have its own set of vanishing points.

2. Similarly, if the object you're drawing isn't rectangular, you'll need a new vanishing point for each new angle you introduce.

As you practice 3-D drawing, don't feel you always have to use a ruler. Try sketching in perspective. Play with the concepts. Make mistakes.

Enjoy!

Remember...

Practice

One of the great secrets of our world is that behind every success there's always plenty of practice. The people who do amazing feats of daring, skill, or ingenuity have been practicing, often for much longer than you'd imagine. They've probably failed more often than you can imagine, too, so don't waste time being discouraged. If your drawings don't look exactly the way you'd like them to, especially when you start out with a new idea, figure out what went wrong, and do it again right!

Save your drawings!

Whenever you do a drawing—or even a sketch—put your initials (or autograph!) and date on it. And save it...maybe not until it turns yellow and crumbles to dust, but at least for several months. Sometimes, hiding in your portfolio, they will mysteriously improve! I've seen it happen often with my own drawings, especially the ones I *knew* were no good at all, but kept anyway.

If you don't have your own portfolio, here's an idea of how you might make one for yourself (you can find a fancy one at an art supply store if you'd rather):

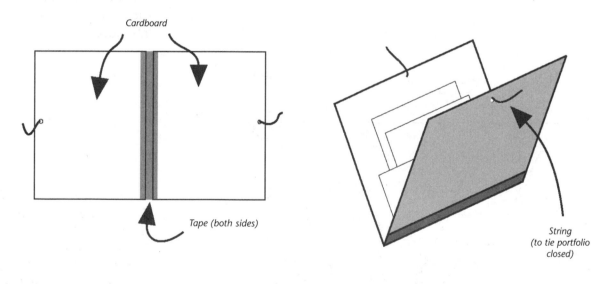

Cardboard

Tape (both sides)

String
(to tie portfolio closed)

To learn about our other books, please visit *drawbooks.com*